No, you can't.

The Left can't meme.

kek

Kek

Kek

kek

Kek

kek

Kek

kek

Kek

kek

Kek

Kek

kek

Kek

kek

Kek

kek

Kek

kek

Kek

Kek

kek

Kek

kek

Kek

kek

Kek

kek

Kek

Kek

kek

Kek

kek

Kek

kek

Kek

kek

Kek

Kek

kek

Kek

kek

Kek

kek

Kek

kek

Kek

Kek

kek

Kek

kek

Kek

kek

Kek

kek

Kek

Kek

kek

Kek

kek

Kek

kek

Kek

kek

Kek

Kek

kek

Kek

kek

Kek

kek

Kek

kek

Kek

Kek

kek

Kek

kek

Kek

kek

Kek

kek

Kek

Kek

kek

Kek

kek

Kek

kek

Kek

kek

Kek

Kek

kek

Kek

kek

Kek

kek

Kek

kek

Kek

Kek

kek

Kek

kek

Kek

kek

Kek

kek

Kek

Kek

kek

Kek

kek

Kek

kek

Kek

kek

Kek

Kek

kek

Kek

kek

Kek

kek

Kek

kek

Kek

Kek

kek

Kek

kek

Kek

kek

Kek

kek

Kek

Kek

kek

Kek

kek

Kek

kek

Kek

kek

Kek

Kek

kek

Kek

kek

Kek

kek

Kek

kek

Kek

Kek

kek

Kek

kek

Kek

kek

Kek

'To show a regressive leftist how to meme is to show a dog a card trick.'

-The Almighty Lord Kek

The End

Made in the USA
Las Vegas, NV
15 January 2022